CONTENTS

Words that appear **in bold** are explained in the glossary.

Copyright © **ticktock Entertainment Ltd 2008**
First published in Great Britain in 2008 by **ticktock Media Ltd.**,
Unit 2, Orchard Business Centre, North Farm Road,
Tunbridge Wells, Kent, TN2 3XF
ISBN 978 1 84696 781 8 pbk
Printed in China

*We would like to thank Penny Worms, our consultants: The International Rhino Foundation - www.rhinos-
irf.org/savetherhinos and the National Literacy Trust.*

Picture credits: t=top, b=bottom, c=centre, l=left, r=right
Corbis: 1, 2, 9, 14, 15, 18, 19, 22-23, 25, 27, 28, 29, 31, 32. Oxford Scientific Photo Library: 8b.
Shutterstock: OFC, 4-5, 6-7, 8t, 10-11, 12-13, 16-17, 20-21, 22-23, 26. Superstock: 7b, 10, 17t.
Every effort has been made to trace the copyright holders, and we apologise in advance for any unintentional omissions. We would be
pleased to insert the appropriate acknowledgements in any subsequent edition of this publication.

AN ANIMAL IN DANGER

Rhino is short for rhinoceros, which means 'nose horn'.

African rhinos live on the grassy plains of southern Africa. Asian rhinos live in forests and on grasslands of Asia and South-east Asia.

Animal experts believe that 200 years ago there were over one million rhinos in the world.

Now there are fewer than 18,700. Some are in danger of disappearing completely.

An Asian female rhinoceros and her calf.

I love reading

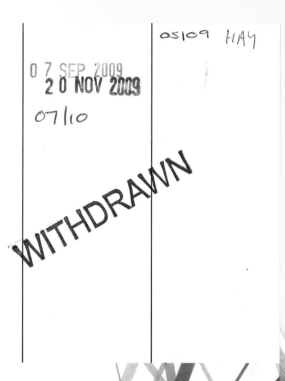

Get **more** out of libraries

Please return or renew this item by the last date shown.
You can renew online at www.hants.gov.uk/library
Or by phoning 0845 603 5631

Hampshire
County Council

ticktock

An African bull
(male) rhinoceros.

AFRICAN RHINOS

There are two types of African rhinos, the Black rhino and the White rhino. Both types are actually grey!

African rhinos live in eastern and southern Africa on open plains.

AFRICA

N
W   E
S

White rhinos have wider mouths than Black rhinos. People who came to Africa thought the local people said *white*, not wide, and this is how they got their name.

An African White rhino

BLACK RHINO FACT

Black rhinos are the rarest African rhino. Most live in **wildlife reserves** where they are protected. Otherwise, they would disappear very quickly.

ASIAN RHINOS

There are three types of rhinos living in Asia. These are the Indian, Sumatran and Javan rhinos.

Indian rhinos live in open places near rivers in northern India and Nepal.

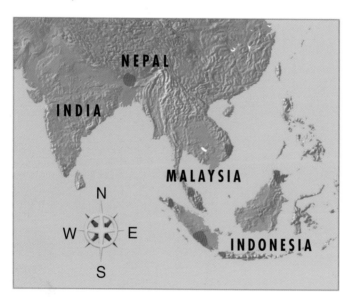

The Sumatran and Javan rhinos live in swamps and forests in Nepal, Malaysia and Indonesia. The Sumatran rhino is sometimes called the hairy rhinoceros because it has a shaggy coat of hair.

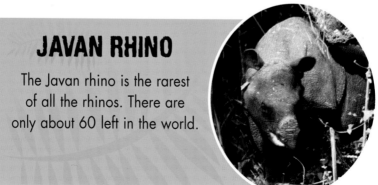

JAVAN RHINO

The Javan rhino is the rarest of all the rhinos. There are only about 60 left in the world.

An Indian rhino

A Sumatran rhino

FEEDING

All rhinos eat plants, but they eat in different ways.

Grazers, such as the White rhinos in this picture, eat grass and other plants found on the ground.

Browsers, like the Black rhino, eat leaves growing on bushes and trees.

Grazers and browsers have different shaped mouths. Wide mouths are good for grazing. Narrow, pointed lips are best for browsing.

A Black rhino's mouth is the right shape for browsing.

RHINO LIFE

Adult rhinos usually live alone. They come together for mating. Sometimes White rhinos will gather where there is lots of food or water.

If you see a group of rhinos, it will probably be a mother with her young, or a group of females, as in this picture.

Male rhinos have **territories**. They mark them with piles of dung. Sometimes these are a metre high! This is a warning to other male rhinos to stay away.

Male rhinos will fight other males that come into their territory.

CHARGING RHINOS

Many people think that rhinos are dangerous animals that will charge at people for no reason.

This isn't true. But if a rhino is frightened, it can run fast – up to 50 kilometres an hour!

A White rhino with her calf.

White and Indian rhino calves usually run in front of their mothers. Black, Javan and Sumatran rhino calves run behind.

PROBLEMS FOR RHINOS - HORNS

Black and White rhinos and Sumatran rhinos have two horns. Indian and Javan rhinos have one horn.

Male rhinos use their horns to fight for territory. The front horn can grow to 1.3 metres long.

Many rhinos have been killed for their horns. **Poaching** is the main reason why these animals are endangered.

Some people believe that rhino horn can cure illnesses – but this isn't true! Others use it to make dagger handles.

RHINO HORN

Rhino horns are made of keratin – the same stuff as your fingernails. Like your fingernails, rhino horns are no use in medicine at all!

Rhinos in a wildlife reserve with a park warden.

18

PROBLEMS FOR RHINOS - HABITAT LOSS

In Africa and Asia the number of people is growing. More land is needed to grow food for them.

Rhinos need a large area of land to find enough food to eat. Their **habitat** is being turned into farmland.

Most rhinos now have to live in protected **wildlife reserves**.

In Asia, the Sumatran rhinos are losing their forests. They are being cut down by **illegal loggers**.

PROBLEMS FOR RHINOS – CLIMATE CHANGE

The changing climate could be a big problem for rhinos and other wild animals.

Climate change can cause **droughts**. Rhinos are put at risk if they have to travel long distances to find water. They might not find enough to survive!

When there is less rain, it affects the plants that grow. In Africa, the grasses that some rhinos eat might be replaced by scrubby bushes.

Less rain also means that desert areas will get bigger.

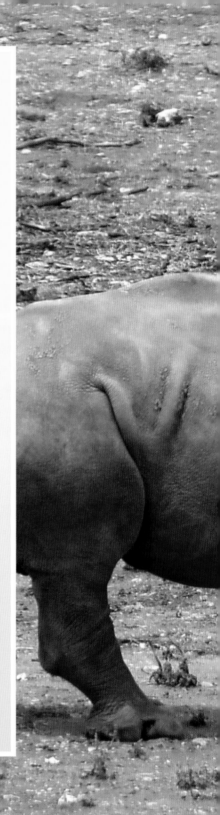

SAVING THE RHINO

People are trying very hard to save the rhino.

Zoos around the world have set up **breeding programmes**. In Africa and Asia wildlife reserves are meant to be safe homes for rhinos. Even so, poaching still happens.

Wildlife tourism helps the rhino. **Tourists** bring in money for the local area. This makes protecting the rhinos more important to local people.

GLOSSARY

breeding programmes Zoos keep rare animals. They help them breed by giving them mates and they help to look after the babies. Some rhinos are put back into the wild, if it is safe.

climate change When the weather in an area changes and stays changed.

droughts When there is no rain for a very long time.

habitat The place that suits a particular wild animal or plant.

illegal loggers People who cut down trees without permission to sell them for wood. They destroy large areas of forest habitat.

poaching The illegal capturing or killing of animals by poachers.

territories Areas of land that an animal believes is its own home and its area for finding its food.

tourists People who are on holiday.

wildlife reserves Places set aside for wild animals and plants to live. The animals and their habitat are protected by laws.

INDEX